Guide Me Day by Day

Inspirational Daily Planner

Activinotes

Activinotes

DAILY JOURNALS, PLANNERS, NOTEBOOKS AND OTHER BLANK BOOKS

Inspirational
Daily Planner

things to do:

The best and most
beautiful things in
the world cannot be
seen or even touched,
they must be felt
with the heart.

Helen Keller

Time	Task Performed	Requested By	Comments	Status

Inspirational
Daily Planner

things to do:

I can't change the
direction of the wind,
but I can adjust my
sails to always reach
my destination.

Jimmy Dean

Time	Task Performed	Requested By	Comments	Status

Inspirational
Daily Planner

things to do:

Start by doing what's
necessary; then do
what's possible; and
suddenly you are doing
the impossible.

Francis of Assisi

Time	Task Performed	Requested By	Comments	Status

Inspirational
Daily Planner

things to do:

Nothing is impossible,
the word itself says '
I'm possible'!

Audrey Hepburn

Time	Task Performed	Requested By	Comments	Status

Inspirational
Daily Planner

things to do:

No act of kindness,
no matter how small,
is ever wasted.

Aesop

Time	Task Performed	Requested By	Comments	Status

Inspirational
Daily Planner

things to do:

I hated every minute of training, but I said, 'Don't quit. Suffer now and live the rest of your life as a champion.'

Muhammad Ali

Time	Task Performed	Requested By	Comments	Status

Inspirational
Daily Planner

things to do:

Happiness is not
something you
postpone for the
future; it is something
you design for the
present.

Jim Rohn

_____ ☐
_____ ☐
_____ ☐
_____ ☐
_____ ☐
_____ ☐
_____ ☐
_____ ☐

Time	Task Performed	Requested By	Comments	Status

Inspirational
Daily Planner

things to do:

The measure of who
we are is what we do
with what we have.

Vince Lombardi

Time	Task Performed	Requested By	Comments	Status

Inspirational
Daily Planner

things to do:

What lies behind you and what lies in front of you, pales in comparison to what lies inside of you.

Ralph Waldo Emerson

_____	☐
_____	☐
_____	☐
_____	☐
_____	☐
_____	☐
_____	☐
_____	☐

Time	Task Performed	Requested By	Comments	Status

Inspirational
Daily Planner

things to do:

Don't judge each day
by the harvest you
reap but by the seeds
that you plant.

Robert Louis Stevenson

Time	Task Performed	Requested By	Comments	Status

Inspirational
Daily Planner

things to do:

Your big opportunity
may be right where
you are now.

Napoleon Hill

☐
☐
☐
☐
☐
☐
☐
☐
☐

Time	Task Performed	Requested By	Comments	Status

Inspirational
Daily Planner

things to do:

The best and most
beautiful things in
the world cannot be
seen or even touched,
they must be felt
with the heart.

Helen Keller

Time	Task Performed	Requested By	Comments	Status

Inspirational
Daily Planner

things to do:

I can't change the
direction of the wind,
but I can adjust my
sails to always reach
my destination.

Jimmy Dean

_____	☐
_____	☐
_____	☐
_____	☐
_____	☐
_____	☐
_____	☐
_____	☐

Time	Task Performed	Requested By	Comments	Status

Inspirational
Daily Planner

things to do:

Start by doing what's
necessary; then do
what's possible; and
suddenly you are doing
the impossible.

Francis of Assisi

Time	Task Performed	Requested By	Comments	Status

Inspirational
Daily Planner

things to do:

Nothing is impossible,
the word itself says
I'm possible!

Audrey Hepburn

_____ ☐
_____ ☐
_____ ☐
_____ ☐
_____ ☐
_____ ☐
_____ ☐
_____ ☐

Time	Task Performed	Requested By	Comments	Status

Inspirational
Daily Planner

things to do:

No act of kindness,
no matter how small,
is ever wasted.

Aesop

Time	Task Performed	Requested By	Comments	Status

Inspirational
Daily Planner

things to do:

I hated every minute
of training, but I said,
'Don't quit. Suffer now
and live the rest of
your life as a champion.'

Muhammad Ali

Time	Task Performed	Requested By	Comments	Status

Inspirational
Daily Planner

things to do:

Happiness is not
something you
postpone for the
future; it is something
you design for the
present.

Jim Rohn

Time	Task Performed	Requested By	Comments	Status

Inspirational
Daily Planner

things to do:

The measure of who
we are is what we do
with what we have.

Vince Lombardi

Time	Task Performed	Requested By	Comments	Status

Inspirational
Daily Planner

things to do:

What lies behind you and what lies in front of you, pales in comparison to what lies inside of you.

Ralph Waldo Emerson

Time	Task Performed	Requested By	Comments	Status

Inspirational
Daily Planner

things to do:

Don't judge each day
by the harvest you
reap but by the seeds
that you plant.

Robert Louis Stevenson

Time	Task Performed	Requested By	Comments	Status

Inspirational
Daily Planner

Your big opportunity may be right where you are now.

Napoleon Hill

things to do:

_____ ☐
_____ ☐
_____ ☐
_____ ☐
_____ ☐
_____ ☐
_____ ☐
_____ ☐

Time	Task Performed	Requested By	Comments	Status

Inspirational Daily Planner

things to do:

The best and most
beautiful things in
the world cannot be
seen or even touched,
they must be felt
with the heart.

Helen Keller

Time	Task Performed	Requested By	Comments	Status

Inspirational
Daily Planner

things to do:

I can't change the
direction of the wind,
but I can adjust my
sails to always reach
my destination.

Jimmy Dean

Time	Task Performed	Requested By	Comments	Status

Inspirational
Daily Planner

things to do:

Start by doing what's
necessary; then do
what's possible; and
suddenly you are doing
the impossible.

Francis of Assisi

Time	Task Performed	Requested By	Comments	Status

Inspirational
Daily Planner

things to do:

**Nothing is impossible,
the word itself says '
I'm possible'!**

Audrey Hepburn

Time	Task Performed	Requested By	Comments	Status

Inspirational
Daily Planner

things to do:

No act of kindness,
no matter how small,
is ever wasted.

Aesop

Time	Task Performed	Requested By	Comments	Status

Inspirational
Daily Planner

things to do:

I hated every minute
of training, but I said,
'Don't quit. Suffer now
and live the rest of
your life as a champion.'

Muhammad Ali

Time	Task Performed	Requested By	Comments	Status

Inspirational
Daily Planner

things to do:

Happiness is not
something you
postpone for the
future; it is something
you design for the
present.

Jim Rohn

Time	Task Performed	Requested By	Comments	Status

Inspirational
Daily Planner

things to do:

The measure of who we are is what we do with what we have.

Vince Lombardi

Time	Task Performed	Requested By	Comments	Status

Inspirational
Daily Planner

things to do:

What lies behind you
and what lies in front
of you, pales in
comparison to what
lies inside of you.

Ralph Waldo Emerson

_____ ☐
_____ ☐
_____ ☐
_____ ☐
_____ ☐
_____ ☐
_____ ☐
_____ ☐

Time	Task Performed	Requested By	Comments	Status

Inspirational Daily Planner

things to do:

Don't judge each day by the harvest you reap but by the seeds that you plant.

Robert Louis Stevenson

_____ ☐
_____ ☐
_____ ☐
_____ ☐
_____ ☐
_____ ☐
_____ ☐
_____ ☐

Time	Task Performed	Requested By	Comments	Status

Inspirational
Daily Planner

things to do:

Your big opportunity
may be right where
you are now.

Napoleon Hill

☐
☐
☐
☐
☐
☐
☐
☐

Time	Task Performed	Requested By	Comments	Status

Inspirational
Daily Planner

things to do:

The best and most
beautiful things in
the world cannot be
seen or even touched,
they must be felt
with the heart.

Helen Keller

Time	Task Performed	Requested By	Comments	Status

Inspirational
Daily Planner

things to do:

I can't change the
direction of the wind,
but I can adjust my
sails to always reach
my destination.

Jimmy Dean

Time	Task Performed	Requested By	Comments	Status

Inspirational
Daily Planner

things to do:

Start by doing what's
necessary; then do
what's possible; and
suddenly you are doing
the impossible.

Francis of Assisi

Time	Task Performed	Requested By	Comments	Status

Inspirational
Daily Planner

things to do:

Nothing is impossible,
the word itself says '
I'm possible'!

Audrey Hepburn

Time	Task Performed	Requested By	Comments	Status

Inspirational
Daily Planner

things to do:

**No act of kindness,
no matter how small,
is ever wasted.**

Aesop

Time	Task Performed	Requested By	Comments	Status

Inspirational
Daily Planner

things to do:

I hated every minute
of training, but I said,
'Don't quit. Suffer now
and live the rest of
your life as a champion.'

Muhammad Ali

Time	Task Performed	Requested By	Comments	Status

Inspirational
Daily Planner

things to do:

Happiness is not
something you
postpone for the
future; it is something
you design for the
present.

Jim Rohn

Time	Task Performed	Requested By	Comments	Status

Inspirational
Daily Planner

things to do:

The measure of who
we are is what we do
with what we have.

Vince Lombardi

Time	Task Performed	Requested By	Comments	Status

Inspirational
Daily Planner

things to do:

What lies behind you
and what lies in front
of you, pales in
comparison to what
lies inside of you.

Ralph Waldo Emerson

———————————— ☐
———————————— ☐
———————————— ☐
———————————— ☐
———————————— ☐
———————————— ☐
———————————— ☐
———————————— ☐

Time	Task Performed	Requested By	Comments	Status

Inspirational
Daily Planner

things to do:

Don't judge each day
by the harvest you
reap but by the seeds
that you plant.

Robert Louis Stevenson

Time	Task Performed	Requested By	Comments	Status

Inspirational
Daily Planner

things to do:

Your big opportunity may be right where you are now.

Napoleon Hill

Time	Task Performed	Requested By	Comments	Status

Inspirational
Daily Planner

The best and most
beautiful things in
the world cannot be
seen or even touched,
they must be felt
with the heart.

Helen Keller

things to do:

_____ ☐
_____ ☐
_____ ☐
_____ ☐
_____ ☐
_____ ☐
_____ ☐
_____ ☐

Time	Task Performed	Requested By	Comments	Status

Inspirational
Daily Planner

things to do:

I can't change the
direction of the wind,
but I can adjust my
sails to always reach
my destination.

Jimmy Dean

Time	Task Performed	Requested By	Comments	Status

Inspirational
Daily Planner

things to do:

Start by doing what's necessary; then do what's possible; and suddenly you are doing the impossible.

Francis of Assisi

_____	☐
_____	☐
_____	☐
_____	☐
_____	☐
_____	☐
_____	☐
_____	☐

Time	Task Performed	Requested By	Comments	Status

Inspirational
Daily Planner

things to do:

**Nothing is impossible,
the word itself says
I'm possible!**

Audrey Hepburn

Time	Task Performed	Requested By	Comments	Status

Inspirational
Daily Planner

things to do:

No act of kindness,
no matter how small,
is ever wasted.

Aesop

Time	Task Performed	Requested By	Comments	Status

Inspirational
Daily Planner

things to do:

I hated every minute
of training, but I said,
'Don't quit. Suffer now
and live the rest of
your life as a champion.'

Muhammad Ali

Time	Task Performed	Requested By	Comments	Status

Inspirational
Daily Planner

things to do:

Happiness is not
something you
postpone for the
future; it is something
you design for the
present.

Jim Rohn

Time	Task Performed	Requested By	Comments	Status

Inspirational
Daily Planner

The measure of who
we are is what we do
with what we have.

Vince Lombardi

things to do:

_____ ☐
_____ ☐
_____ ☐
_____ ☐
_____ ☐
_____ ☐
_____ ☐
_____ ☐

Time	Task Performed	Requested By	Comments	Status

Inspirational
Daily Planner

things to do:

What lies behind you
and what lies in front
of you, pales in
comparison to what
lies inside of you.

Ralph Waldo Emerson

Time	Task Performed	Requested By	Comments	Status

Inspirational
Daily Planner

things to do:

Don't judge each day
by the harvest you
reap but by the seeds
that you plant.

Robert Louis Stevenson

Time	Task Performed	Requested By	Comments	Status

Inspirational
Daily Planner

things to do:

Your big opportunity
may be right where
you are now.

Napoleon Hill

Time	Task Performed	Requested By	Comments	Status

Inspirational
Daily Planner

things to do:

The best and most
beautiful things in
the world cannot be
seen or even touched,
they must be felt
with the heart.

Helen Keller

Time	Task Performed	Requested By	Comments	Status

Inspirational
Daily Planner

things to do:

I can't change the
direction of the wind,
but I can adjust my
sails to always reach
my destination.

Jimmy Dean

_____ ☐
_____ ☐
_____ ☐
_____ ☐
_____ ☐
_____ ☐
_____ ☐
_____ ☐

Time	Task Performed	Requested By	Comments	Status

Inspirational
Daily Planner

things to do:

Start by doing what's necessary; then do what's possible; and suddenly you are doing the impossible.

Francis of Assisi

Time	Task Performed	Requested By	Comments	Status

Inspirational
Daily Planner

things to do:

**Nothing is impossible,
the word itself says '
I'm possible'!**

Audrey Hepburn

Time	Task Performed	Requested By	Comments	Status

Inspirational
Daily Planner

things to do:

**No act of kindness,
no matter how small,
is ever wasted.**

Aesop

Time	Task Performed	Requested By	Comments	Status

Inspirational
Daily Planner

things to do:

I hated every minute
of training, but I said,
'Don't quit. Suffer now
and live the rest of
your life as a champion.'

Muhammad Ali

Time	Task Performed	Requested By	Comments	Status

Inspirational
Daily Planner

things to do:

Happiness is not
something you
postpone for the
future; it is something
you design for the
present.

Jim Rohn

_____ ☐
_____ ☐
_____ ☐
_____ ☐
_____ ☐
_____ ☐
_____ ☐
_____ ☐

Time	Task Performed	Requested By	Comments	Status

Inspirational
Daily Planner

things to do:

The measure of who
we are is what we do
with what we have.

Vince Lombardi

Time	Task Performed	Requested By	Comments	Status

Inspirational Daily Planner

things to do:

What lies behind you and what lies in front of you, pales in comparison to what lies inside of you.

Ralph Waldo Emerson

Time	Task Performed	Requested By	Comments	Status

Inspirational
Daily Planner

things to do:

Don't judge each day
by the harvest you
reap but by the seeds
that you plant.

Robert Louis Stevenson

Time	Task Performed	Requested By	Comments	Status

Inspirational
Daily Planner

things to do:

Your big opportunity
may be right where
you are now.

Napoleon Hill

☐
☐
☐
☐
☐
☐
☐
☐

Time	Task Performed	Requested By	Comments	Status

Inspirational
Daily Planner

things to do:

The best and most
beautiful things in
the world cannot be
seen or even touched,
they must be felt
with the heart.

Helen Keller

Time	Task Performed	Requested By	Comments	Status

Inspirational
Daily Planner

things to do:

I can't change the
direction of the wind,
but I can adjust my
sails to always reach
my destination.

Jimmy Dean

Time	Task Performed	Requested By	Comments	Status

Inspirational
Daily Planner

things to do:

Start by doing what's
necessary; then do
what's possible; and
suddenly you are doing
the impossible.

Francis of Assisi

Time	Task Performed	Requested By	Comments	Status

Inspirational
Daily Planner

things to do:

Nothing is impossible,
the word itself says '
I'm possible'!

Audrey Hepburn

Time	Task Performed	Requested By	Comments	Status

Inspirational
Daily Planner

things to do:

No act of kindness,
no matter how small,
is ever wasted.

Aesop

_____ ☐
_____ ☐
_____ ☐
_____ ☐
_____ ☐
_____ ☐
_____ ☐
_____ ☐

Time	Task Performed	Requested By	Comments	Status

Inspirational Daily Planner

things to do:

I hated every minute
of training, but I said,
'Don't quit. Suffer now
and live the rest of
your life as a champion.'

Muhammad Ali

Time	Task Performed	Requested By	Comments	Status

Inspirational Daily Planner

things to do:

Happiness is not
something you
postpone for the
future; it is something
you design for the
present.

Jim Rohn

Time	Task Performed	Requested By	Comments	Status

Inspirational
Daily Planner

things to do:

The measure of who we are is what we do with what we have.

Vince Lombardi

Time	Task Performed	Requested By	Comments	Status

Inspirational
Daily Planner

things to do:

What lies behind you
and what lies in front
of you, pales in
comparison to what
lies inside of you.

Ralph Waldo Emerson

_____ ☐
_____ ☐
_____ ☐
_____ ☐
_____ ☐
_____ ☐
_____ ☐
_____ ☐

Time	Task Performed	Requested By	Comments	Status

Inspirational
Daily Planner

things to do:

Don't judge each day
by the harvest you
reap but by the seeds
that you plant.

Robert Louis Stevenson

Time	Task Performed	Requested By	Comments	Status

Inspirational
Daily Planner

things to do:

Your big opportunity
may be right where
you are now.

Napoleon Hill

Time	Task Performed	Requested By	Comments	Status

Inspirational
Daily Planner

The best and most
beautiful things in
the world cannot be
seen or even touched,
they must be felt
with the heart.

Helen Keller

things to do:

_____ ☐
_____ ☐
_____ ☐
_____ ☐
_____ ☐
_____ ☐
_____ ☐
_____ ☐

Time	Task Performed	Requested By	Comments	Status

Inspirational
Daily Planner

things to do:

I can't change the
direction of the wind,
but I can adjust my
sails to always reach
my destination.

Jimmy Dean

Time	Task Performed	Requested By	Comments	Status

Inspirational
Daily Planner

things to do:

Start by doing what's
necessary; then do
what's possible; and
suddenly you are doing
the impossible.

Francis of Assisi

Time	Task Performed	Requested By	Comments	Status

Inspirational
Daily Planner

things to do:

Nothing is impossible, _____ ☐
the word itself says ' _____ ☐
I'm possible'! _____ ☐
_____ ☐
Audrey Hepburn _____ ☐
_____ ☐
_____ ☐
_____ ☐

Time	Task Performed	Requested By	Comments	Status

Inspirational
Daily Planner

things to do:

No act of kindness,
no matter how small,
is ever wasted.

Aesop

Time	Task Performed	Requested By	Comments	Status

Inspirational
Daily Planner

things to do:

I hated every minute
of training, but I said,
'Don't quit. Suffer now
and live the rest of
your life as a champion.'

Muhammad Ali

Time	Task Performed	Requested By	Comments	Status

Inspirational
Daily Planner

things to do:

Happiness is not
something you
postpone for the
future; it is something
you design for the
present.

Jim Rohn

Time	Task Performed	Requested By	Comments	Status

Inspirational
Daily Planner

things to do:

The measure of who
we are is what we do
with what we have.

Vince Lombardi

Time	Task Performed	Requested By	Comments	Status

Inspirational
Daily Planner

things to do:

What lies behind you
and what lies in front
of you, pales in
comparison to what
lies inside of you.

Ralph Waldo Emerson

Time	Task Performed	Requested By	Comments	Status

Inspirational
Daily Planner

things to do:

Don't judge each day
by the harvest you
reap but by the seeds
that you plant.

Robert Louis Stevenson

_____ ☐
_____ ☐
_____ ☐
_____ ☐
_____ ☐
_____ ☐
_____ ☐
_____ ☐

Time	Task Performed	Requested By	Comments	Status

Inspirational
Daily Planner

things to do:

Your big opportunity
may be right where
you are now.

Napoleon Hill

Time	Task Performed	Requested By	Comments	Status

Inspirational
Daily Planner

things to do:

The best and most
beautiful things in
the world cannot be
seen or even touched,
they must be felt
with the heart.

Helen Keller

Time	Task Performed	Requested By	Comments	Status

Inspirational
Daily Planner

things to do:

I can't change the
direction of the wind,
but I can adjust my
sails to always reach
my destination.

Jimmy Dean

Time	Task Performed	Requested By	Comments	Status

Inspirational
Daily Planner

things to do:

Start by doing what's necessary; then do what's possible; and suddenly you are doing the impossible.

Francis of Assisi

Time	Task Performed	Requested By	Comments	Status

Inspirational Daily Planner

things to do:

Nothing is impossible,
the word itself says '
I'm possible'!

Audrey Hepburn

Time	Task Performed	Requested By	Comments	Status

Inspirational
Daily Planner

things to do:

No act of kindness,
no matter how small,
is ever wasted.

Aesop

Time	Task Performed	Requested By	Comments	Status

Inspirational
Daily Planner

things to do:

I hated every minute
of training, but I said,
'Don't quit. Suffer now
and live the rest of
your life as a champion.'

Muhammad Ali

Time	Task Performed	Requested By	Comments	Status

Inspirational
Daily Planner

things to do:

Happiness is not
something you
postpone for the
future; it is something
you design for the
present.

Jim Rohn

Time	Task Performed	Requested By	Comments	Status

Inspirational
Daily Planner

The measure of who
we are is what we do
with what we have.

Vince Lombardi

things to do:

Time	Task Performed	Requested By	Comments	Status

Inspirational
Daily Planner

things to do:

What lies behind you
and what lies in front
of you, pales in
comparison to what
lies inside of you.

Ralph Waldo Emerson

_____ ☐
_____ ☐
_____ ☐
_____ ☐
_____ ☐
_____ ☐
_____ ☐
_____ ☐

Time	Task Performed	Requested By	Comments	Status

Inspirational
Daily Planner

things to do:

Don't judge each day
by the harvest you
reap but by the seeds
that you plant.

Robert Louis Stevenson

Time	Task Performed	Requested By	Comments	Status

Inspirational Daily Planner

Your big opportunity may be right where you are now.

Napoleon Hill

things to do:

_____ ☐
_____ ☐
_____ ☐
_____ ☐
_____ ☐
_____ ☐
_____ ☐
_____ ☐

Time	Task Performed	Requested By	Comments	Status

Inspirational
Daily Planner

things to do:

The best and most
beautiful things in
the world cannot be
seen or even touched,
they must be felt
with the heart.

Helen Keller

Time	Task Performed	Requested By	Comments	Status

Inspirational
Daily Planner

things to do:

I can't change the
direction of the wind,
but I can adjust my
sails to always reach
my destination.

Jimmy Dean

Time	Task Performed	Requested By	Comments	Status

Inspirational
Daily Planner

things to do:

Start by doing what's
necessary; then do
what's possible; and
suddenly you are doing
the impossible.

Francis of Assisi

Time	Task Performed	Requested By	Comments	Status

Inspirational
Daily Planner

things to do:

Nothing is impossible, the word itself says 'I'm possible'!

Audrey Hepburn

			□
			□
			□
			□
			□
			□
			□
			□

Time	Task Performed	Requested By	Comments	Status

Inspirational
Daily Planner

things to do:

No act of kindness,
no matter how small,
is ever wasted.

Aesop

Time	Task Performed	Requested By	Comments	Status

www.ingramcontent.com/pod-product-compliance
Lightning Source LLC
Chambersburg PA
CBHW080737250626
47170CB00010B/2856